HUMOR AND GRIPES
A collection of poems and Short Essays

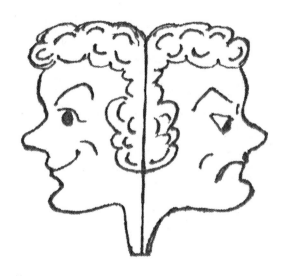

By
Alva Houston

PublishAmerica
Baltimore

First printing

At the specific preference of the author, PublishAmerica allowed this work to remain exactly as the author intended, verbatim, without editorial input.

ISBN: 1-4137-7994-8
PUBLISHED BY PUBLISHAMERICA, LLLP
www.publishamerica.com
Baltimore

Printed in the United States of America

I would like to dedicate it to Cal Burrows, my first love,
who died in the Normandy invasion....WW2

CONTENTS

1.
A little about Doug and Myself

After retiring from two jobs and playing piano bar at night I found that it was a great release to paint and write. Living in other countries gave me opinions about my own that I may never have entertained had I stayed stateside! I lived in China and South Africa as I have said before.

I have been told by many that I am an opinionated old lady…and I admit it. By the time you hit 79 I believe you have a right to strong opinions, and if you don't have any you are just a blob! Either that or you have been brainwashed by the TV and can not think for yourself!

Living with others is at best a real test of patience, which I am rather short of. Doug and I get along because our interests coincide. We can be ourselves and even have hearty arguments at times. Never really holding grudges is the way it works for us. After all, we are imperfect humans. One advantage we have now that we are old is that we can get up anytime we want to and not have to face an unpleasant boss! We have been blessed to be raised in the greatest country in the world and have been free! It looks as if that freedom is going down the drain and that is part of the reason why I write! It helps let loose my frustrations on a piece of paper.....rather than taking them out through violence of some kind!

Believe me there are senators and congress men and woman whom I should love to slap across their mouths, but darn it…I'll never get the chance.

Written 4/13/2005
By Alva Houston

2.
ADVICE TO YOUNG PEOPLE

Even if no young person reads this it does me good to give advice from an elderly lady, having lived almost 79 years!

When I was young I thought a lot about old age and dying. Having seen my dear Grandma Houston lying in death it really made an impression on me.

I think if young people thought about these things they might live differently...not doing everything their selfishness demands! We are all imperfect and selfish just being humans.

Unfortunately in todays' world it seems as if sex, comforts and money are more important to the average person than living right! By that I mean that considering others and giving of yourself is not a priority.

I'm glad I'm old and will not be around when the curtain closes upon our taken for granted freedoms. I fear that this is fast approaching and few seem to care.

Individuals are shoved to the background and group-think holds sway. Every great invention in history came about through the effort and genious of individuals! We are on the slippery slope to the dark ages all over again because we refuse to face the facts that stare us in the face every day. Judges, politicians and a shadowy group behind them are in command and intent us to be just another third world nation that they can control. There is one flaw in their plans. That is: Who will pay for all their evil plans when the working man is broke and can't pay taxes? That is "Killing the Goose that layed the Golden Egg"...is it not?

A WISE AFRIKAANER

An Afrikaaner is a person who comes from Dutch-German roots and lives in South Africa. I lived there for 7 years and learned a lot from these wonderful settlers. One man inparticular talked about ideas and pretty deep subjects…he was from that lineage.

He used to say,"never trust an animal or a person who shows the whites of their eyes a lot! That made me think of Hillary Clinton, Barbara Pelosi, and Mara Liasson of public radio fame. All are liberals and opinionated women for their cause…internationalizing our country!

The voices that cry out for our remaining a sovereign Republic (we are NOT a democracy. That is the misnaming of our country for political purposes, I believe.) are very few, because the media is liberal and never allows too many of us (who are conservatives) any time to express our views.

Even though we are old, my husband Doug and I keep on talking about what we see as the dangerous direction the liberal thinkers are heading and have been heading our country for more than fifty years. Most people do not want their comfort zone disturbed and will not discuss the subject. That is how much we have been brainwashed! The tragedy is that future generations will be led like sheep, and the Jews in WW2 to their own destruction.

We are fast becoming a "Controlled people" who are weak and gutless, have few morals, and worst of all are full of fear! What ever happened to those who had principles and were unafraid to stand up for freedom…not for one group or other, but for the individual? We sorely need a lot of "Bravehearts" in our country who are not afraid of dying for freedom if necessary!

Written 7/29/2004 by Alva Houston

MOTHER

I don't think anyone ever understood my mother. She kept all feelings inside herself, and with others didn't bother.

She had one real interest in her life. Golf was her therapy, and something she did very well and important she could be!

I think my trying to please her for a lifetime was so wrong. I did try as I loved her, but she sang a different song.

I cared for her and my dad for years alone and am glad that I did it though lots of times I was very sad!
I bathed and fed and nurtured the best that I could do. I feel good about it now, but my advice to you, (who read this heartfelt poem), is please don't do what I DO!

The stress is really too much for a person to take on…and nobody will give you thanks until you're finally gone.

ANIMAL FRIENDS

Just because you get old doesn't mean you become wise! Some people learn from their experiences what love and hate mean. Others plod along through life nurturing their prejudices, trained ideas, and hatreds until they die. Love always works better in the long run, although I admit it really is a hard struggle to learn "unconditional love".

I like to use animals I have known as examples of the ideal! Although they can't speak in our terms, or work with their hands the same way we do, our domesticated friends show us everyday how unconditional love works! This is with one notable exception. If you don't feed them and give a bit of affection to them, they may not follow the rules.

I have found over 78 years that animals are honest, loyal and show amazing intelligence that they are often not given credit for. Just having a dog, cat, horse or bird around is good for you in many ways. Here are ten ways they add to the richness of life.

They force you to get off your behind and let them out when they need to go potty. (Good for old people to keep them alert and moving)
They ask for food if you forget to feed them or leave it in their dish! Cats especially, demand that their dish be full and not half empty!
They are always glad to see you when you come home.
They have completely different personalities just as humans do…BUT
They learn to "get along" despite their differences!
They seem to know when danger is at hand.
They warn you when people knock at that door and if they don't like them dogs will defend!
They show forgiveness when you have been stupid and yelled at them.
They curl up with you when you are feeling low or hurt. Even birds do

this if left free in the house.

And last but not least, they are beautiful to look at and want to please you.

We can learn much from our furry and feathered friends if we have the patience to notice their behavior. It oftentimes beats that of humans!

ANOTHER DAY!

Another day has come and gone. It seems they go more quickly. The older you get the more you fret…the more you get real prickly!

When you have lived a long, long time and see the world around you has changed so radically, my friend, and in the end has found you disgusted with many of the ways people live and think…They are immoral and do things perverted without a blink!

If Jerry Springer and Howard Stern can make their audiences happy…I don't see much hope for

Any of us…things are whacky! Rome really had nothing on us…violence, games, and sex they did. Now the USA has become the same. Of this fact we can't be rid. The Bible says that "They love the darkness rather than the light". I believe this is my country's plight!

BEANS

A friend gave me a pot of her baked beans today. The trouble is I ate too much…for this I had to pay! The gas came first and then a nasty accident in my jeans. My Lord how I have suffered and been cleaned out by her beans. I bet I ran to the bathroom a dozen times today. I'll never ask my friend for more. No more, no more I say!

BEEGIE ADAIR

Beegie plays the best piano I have ever heard, so I want to thank for her jazz style. It's the best I've ever heard in a long, long while. She can do it all on the keyboard, but has respect for the original tune. Her humbleness comes through and soon...she will end up in the musicians' hall of fame. Wish that I could say the same.

I want her to know that her piano really keeps me going, in this nutty world where most people don't know what they're sowing! She has sown a garden of tunes with talent that nobody will forget. That I may never meet her is my sincere regret.

BINGO

I played that game of bingo…once!

Let me tell you those gals sitting there, with their pals, are the smartest bunch. I was confused and miserable, and simply "out to lunch".

They played all of these crazy games. I can't remember all the names. I know Bingo's not for me as had a headache finally!

Well, in a while I spent my bucks and ended up with saying "shucks". Bingo's not my game, that's all. I'd rather hit a white golf ball. So I say "viva la difference" for playing golf, to me, makes sense.

Now you may not agree with me, so I thank God that we're still free. Whether we be girl or boy, we still can do things we enjoy!

CASINOS

I meet a lot of people who think Casinos evil. Well, they can be, I admit. There are reasons why folks go there to throw their money in a machine. They are either bored, need to get out of the house, disillusioned with life, lonely, or honestly in need of a large sum to pay bills!

When my Christians friends criticize me for going to our little local casino I tell them, "I believe that is where Jesus would be as he always was with sinners who needed Him, and He called the religious Jewish leadership of the time, "A Den of Vipers" as I remember. How many of the unsaved who may be miserable and lonely will go into a church?

The churches are all divided and have different doctrines and people see that and wonder WHY!
I believe it is because they are all run by men and women who are sinners in the first place.

As the Bible teaches "The Kingdom of God is Within You" not in an institution! LOVE of course is the answer to any problem because it never fails. "GOD IS LOVE", the word teaches,
and that is what I believe and what sustains me.

We all DIE! One hundred years from now there will be few, who live now, left on the planet. If we thought about that fact more I think it would change us for the better. Just imagine if we all followed the teachings of Jesus...no police, no government with armies, nobody ignoring their neighbors needs, the wonderful world of beautiful thoughts and creations and most of all no people who think they are superior to others!

Written in view of the fact that I soon approach the final reality...Death !

CHINA

In 1946 I traveled to China with a four month old baby to meet my husband who was there to work for Standard Vacuum Oil…a Rockefeller company. My experiences taught me about the backward ways of the Chinese. From province to province they couldn't understand each other because of differences in dialects! As with Muslim nations, women were considered inferior to men, and soldiers at the bottom of the barrel. I have written the whole story in "Pre Mau TzeDung".

Those memories come back vividly as I now read about the communist treatment of Christians. They just beat to death a young woman for distributing Bibles. The shame of it all is that we, the USA were the ones responsible for handing over the country to the communists in 1949. After that they managed to murder 30,000,000 people! It was our government who withdrew aid from a good man, Chiang-Kai-Shek leaving him helpless to defend his people. He ended up fleeing to Taiwan. Chiang's wife was educated at an American college and interested in bringing the Chinese up from being controlled for centuries by warlords!

Anyone who thinks the Chinese Communists can be changed by trade is nuts, I think. The country has 1,500,000,000 people and needs land. Who do you think they are looking at? We are paying their way to domination through buying all their goods.

I wish Americans were less naïve and more realistic!

12.
CITIZENS OF THE WORLD

What does this really mean?

Are you also a citizen of Ruanda where 800,000 died as a result of massacres with machetes in a week?

Are you also a citizen of Sudan, where little kids are sold into sexual slavery and are killed by the millions for being Christians?

Are you a citizen of China where you have to abort girl babies and their organs then get sold on the world market?

Are you a citizen of France who we bailed out in WW2 and who has turned on us ever since then?

Are you fond of Germany, who has turned into a socialist nightmare and is almost broke and whose leader, Schroeder, is nothing but a communist thug from East Germany?

Are you a citizen of most Islamic countries who keep the women down and give them clitorectomies so they won't stray?

Are you a citizen of North Korea, where it's people are starving while its' leaders build up their nuclear weapons to attack others?

How about Somalia where we tried with typical American kindness to help the people get out from under a ruthless warlord?

Are you a citizen of Haiti, where they put rubber tires around you, tie down and burn you to death if you oppose the powers that be?

I could go on and on but as a last thought for those who downgrade our President. If you think that our country is to blame for most of the world's ills, be a part of those who leave us and have nothing but criticism to show for where they were born...in the greatest free country in the world! My friends died in wars caused by despots, and they died for you!

CLEANING

Dusting just ain't for me these days. Six animals make it hopeless with the dust they raise! When I was young I ran around looking for cobwebs, by cleanliness bound. Now I dust once a month, when I see much around.

At the advanced age of 78, why should I care
How much dust I just ate! They say you eat bushels of dirt in your lives. It never made ME sick or gave me the hives.

When littles kids crawl all over the floor, that's the time for vacuuming and much more. Thank God they're grown up with hands in their pockets, and not little ones rubbing their mouths and eye sockets.

I think that cleaning is such a real bore for it makes your back ache and your extremities sore!

THE DAY HAS COME

Yes, the day has arrived when the ordinary, tax-paying citizen can no longer protect himself and his family! No-good, welfare collecting men are being moved into good neighborhoods around us and they are causing trouble for everybody who obeys the law.

They come knocking at your door for cigarettes, and money and threaten people who walk down the street in front of their section 8 houses. They are not controlled and probably are parollees.

When you call the police they are never there, and when you do get them they tell you "call us" and don't do anything to protect yourself...some comfort, knowing that we are being looked after by the law!

We have weapons for hunting but are warned never to even threated anyone or we'll end up facing the courts and corrupt judges. Something is terribly wrong here, when a quiet little town becomes a place of harassment and intimidation. The next thing you know we will have to live behind barred windows and doors.

written 8/2004

DEATH

"The Two things we can be sure of are death and taxes", so the old saying goes! The fact is that it can come at any time, whether we are young or old. I believe we should all think about that harsh fact.

Death is not MORBID if you believe that your life has meaning and there is an afterlife. If you don't, you are stuck with the idea that you really mean nothing and are just an accident in the scheme of things. That is MORBID!

I think that the worst of us would live better lives if we DID think a lot about death. For instance, it is wise to consider that we may have to stand before a judgement seat and answer for our lives.

That should be enough to drive us straight into the arms of a loving God. To do otherwise would be taking an awful chance that I, for one, am not willing to take. I'll leave it with Jesus Christ, who put us all on a level playing field. He said we are all sinners and need a Saviour!

DECIPHERING POETRY

When we have to decipher a poem it's wrong! A poem should be understandable and strong.

You should read it with pleasure and sometimes a kick from the humor it brings it will not make you sick. There are those who keep writing from fantasy land. Most have never lived in the real world at hand. They pride themselves always on intellect great, and don't depend on experience that leaves one awake…to life itself treasured from travel and work. They depend on their reading …reality shirk!

They write from what books seems to put in their minds instead of getting experience off their behinds. Now I don't say imaging can't be attractive…it offers a lot to those who aren't active! They seem always wanting to impress those around them, with their knowledge of life and the things that have bound them. I for one thank my maker for talents I own, which have been honed in a lifetime of struggle alone.

I feel sorry for those who's poetry is at hand.
As I read I wonder if they live in La-La land.
For a poem to be great it really must touch the average person deciphering it easily and such.

The great writers have lived a full life in this world and put it all down with their wisdom unfurled.

Now I don't even consider myself in this bunch of the greats, but I'd like to be so very much!

DICTATORSHIP
US Style

We have a dictatorship whether the people of this great country know it or not! When one judge can dictate whether or not a person lives or dies…that, my friend, is dictatorship. Where the Terri Shindler case goes from here when they have killed the woman, is anyone's guess.

I have grave fears that this is just the beginning of getting rid of a lot of people that are costing medicare and social security too much money. I think that's what it is really about.

Waco, Ruby Ridge and Elian Gonsales were the precursers of this movement for euthanasia which is backed by Communists in this country. Hitler was a socialist as well as Stalin and Sadaam Hussein! They never hesitated to get rid of anyone who stood in their way.

Their way was DICTATORSHIP!

DIFFERENT STROKES

I'm sure everyone knows this favorite saying. It is so true that we all see things and hear them differently depending on our prejudices, backgrounds and the teaching we have had. There is one thing that separates Americans from other peoples of this world and that is that they are free to express those opinions we hold dear without being persecuted by the law, thrown in jail or tortured...so far!

Only because of our "value of Freedom" in all it's forms do we Americans get along pretty darn well, and go on to higher ground!

Amongst us there are those, who because of their own narrow mindedess, ignorance or bitterness want to destroy this basic foundation of our Republic. They can't do it only because Americans have a keen sense of right and wrong...most have faith in God and good humor! Humor has saved us many times as we go struggling along fighting for what we believe in...fighting even the wars, the disputes, the agonies of personal attacks upon us and many other difficulties that we face in life.

To keep from falling into the trap of being whiners and complainers Americans have developed a very good sense of humor which sustains them even when life seems hopeless and dark at times.

As we all approach and pass through our latter years, pain, in real forms comes upon us all and that is when great faith and great humor come in handy. Not because of arrogance or my ego I always tell my young compatriots that "You'll get old if you live long enough", with some humor. I know that we all suddenly realize at that stage that something very spiritual is going on throughout our lives. One can't always put a finger on it, but we (most of us) know that this life is NOT for nothing! I get such a thrill when I wake up at all and even in pain, because it tells me I have another day to learn more, pain or not. I'm becoming more convinced that pain, physical or mental is allowed not to be punishment but to heal our basic lack of humility, lack of understanding and of love.

After all, Love seems to be the only thing in life that really matters, works and that giving is a big part of it all. It is the lack of it and meanness that destroys us and a rejection of God. Everything created by that source cannot be copied by any scientist or man, yet all comes from a mysterious source...seeds can't be made by anyone, and are what create every living thing we have and have to live on...even ourselves!

I think of life in terms of genes we're given and have to deal with everywhere as we pass through this life, They certainly do brand us with certain qualities and talents but also need to be contolled. Our different strokes come from our genes and if we are blessed with good ones by our ancestors, we are winners already. If not, we just have to pay attention to our mistakes and get some wisdom from observing this great experience called, LIVING!

written 9/1/2004 by Alva Houston

DOUG

Had it not been for fate I would never have written anything at all!

12 years ago I said a little prayer that if I should have a companion in my old age, he or she would have to enter my life through no effort on my part! Unbelievably my first cousin Doug Kjellmark called me the very next morning. I hadn't seen him for 36 years!

Call it coincidence…I call it a miracle. He lived in Kentucky…I in California. I invited him to visit and he did with the result that we decided to live together and help each other through our old age years.

He has been a great friend throughout these 12 years and I have had support from him in everything I've done in those years! This enabled me to write children's books, an autobiography, draw cartoons for a book of over 100, and paint many oil paintings. I also have created cds of my original music and many recordings. When you have someone behind you in your efforts, it makes such a difference!

Friendship, purely platonic is the path we chose, and it works wonderfully well. We can be true to ourselves. Doug is a fine man and was a fine little boy when we spent summers together on our Uncle Frank's farm. We share a small home together with our beloved 6 animals. We have 4 cats and two dogs. They keep us hopping! Thanks Doug!

DREAMS

Don't you ever wonder if dreams come true?
The truth is, that I certainly do.

I've also been dreaming lately of some dollars coming in, from the sale of my books for children. Is this an awful sin?

I've been writing and been drawing for many many years! And being a natural pessimist I had a lot of fears, that IF my books ever over internet should go, the bucks would go to someone else…posthumously, you know!

EARLY BIRD

I get up in the morning and go to bed the same. I've always been a day person from the moment that I came. I think perhaps it's when you're born that determines how you behave. If you're born early in the day, you'll rise early to the grave.

A painting I just started of Doug and our dog Jake…would like to get a-going, but too much fuss I'd make. I'd have to go to Doug's room and remove things that are there. I guess I'll just get up now and at the walls may stare.

Nothing on the boob tube means much to me anymore. In fact it merely a lot of noise, a constant, restless bore! So guess I'll write this poem and maybe think of things, until the coffee's ready…that each day always brings.

For every day is different and unique in it's own way … just remembered the reality of those bills I have to pay!

EDUCATION?

For fifty years I have had fears since once I was a teacher. I feared that the government was changing our schools and becoming the main preacher….of what is right and what is wrong. I worked hard to discover that the reason the biggies were changing things was to do-in every mother! We'll soon find out …that we allowed these crazy leftists to control most everything. Does what I'm writing to you dear people have a familiar ring.

Hitler and Stalin had the same ideas…to make children robots affected by their peers. They fall in step because they want to be member of a group. An individual stands out and ends up in the soup! Of course this brainwashing always leads to tyranny. I'm glad I'm old and the end of it won't see! It's going to be bloody I fear…that's why I drive facts home…again and again. We on the way to Rome.

The only difference between the fall of Rome and us is this, my friend: They lasted a thousand years and we only had two hundred before the end!

23.

EMOTIONS

They turn us into children with very little real feeling. They make us fools most of the time and send our senses reeling! They make us see reality through glass that is opaque. When we depend on feelings more than brainpower it's a mistake.

We Americans are told and programmed from the morning to the night to depend on "How we feel". This is an awful plight. To think for yourself is not popular, but to be a "groupie" is! To follow like sheep the powers that be is said to be our biz!

God help you if you happen to have a sense of humor clean…one that's not based on dirty words or sex or things obscene. You're simply told to "get along" and forget how you believe, by people in the media who lie and do deceive!

If you lose your right to think and have your own opinions…you lose your freedom and all rights that come from GOD"S dominions!

Written in 2001.

EQUAL?

The Declaration of Independence declares that "All Men are created Equal", yet this is not really true in the sense that we are all created different when it comes to talents, desires, and situations.

What they should have said in my humble opinion is that "all men and women are created equal in having opportunity".

Yet even this is wrong too for most people are limited in the freedom and the money needed to express their lives and demands made on them.

Herein lies the problems facing humankind in 2005 and all the way back through history!

How can we make a world where each individual has a chance to make the most of his or her life? There is absolutely no formula for this. We have watched history try to correct this dilemma by forming institutions. All have failed: Communism, socialism, fascism, progressivism, and capitalism. There is one "ism" which does work, but today it is lost in the shuffle of ideas espoused by the intellectuals on the left! This is "Individualism" which has given us all the inventions of any importance down through the life of the planet! Freedom demands that individuals not be grouped into movements that only serve to divide people! We all must remember that despots and dictators fear individuals more than anything else. They can't control them! When we fall into the trap of group movements be they of the left or right politically, we destroy the ideals which only freedom can bring.

ESSAY ON AGING

As I try to live "one day at a time" I realize the wonders of what God has provided that no woman or man can!

The sun comes up and feeds our plants which in turn feed us.

The night and darkness bring rest and quiet from the cacophony of madness that seems to surround us everyday.

Seeds, which no man has ever made provide a beauty which takes one's breath away!

Friendly pets give comfort and company when you feel alone and nobody seems to care.

The brain keeps plodding along when the body is failing (unless one has Alzheimers disease).

You are given talents from birth which in themselves are a miracle, and you never had anything to do with it.

You know there must be a reason for being here and are comforted by the realization that there is a higher source in charge.

You are lucky enough to live in a country where the average person has more freedom and luxuries that anyone else in the world.

You are fortunate to have had ancestors who left corrupt and decaying countries because they wanted freedom.

You are lucky in that our forefathers left us with a Constitution which has so far protected us from greedy, power-hungry people who wish to rule the earth!

You are blessed by the fact that our country's men and women went to fight for freedom all across the world, and were willing to die for it!

These are all your inheritance.

Just think if people loved each other as they do themselves how we would live without fear, without armies, police and government for that matter!

EXCUSES

This life ain't easy and we all learn, that making excuses for ourselves others spurn! You can blame your ma and pa for your unhappy youth, for your mistakes along life's way and being uncouth. There is another voice that tells you that you are the one who messed up your life or became a bum!

His call is the one many will not receive. It comes straight from God is what I believe. The call is to look to God for understanding and the teachings of Jesus tells us what He's demanding. He tells us to turn to Him before death comes our way…for it's the final arbiter …so trust and obey!

WHY HAVE FEAR?

There are many fears that haunt us throughout our lives, but the biggest one is what will happen before and after our demise!

When you are a kid you fear the dark and imagination sometimes runs wild. Yes, many things are to be feared when you're a child.

When you arrive at puberty there are other fears,
Which attack both you and peers. You have urges to do certain things that nature in her time always brings!

As a mother or father you have lots of fears, that your kids will be hurt by taunts and not cheers.

The real fear should be "Fear of The Lord", which the Bible teaches is the "beginning of Wisdom". Psalm 111:10. We may have to answer for every word and deed before the judgment seat of God, and we really need...to consider this before we die. The Bible speaks truth and doesn't lie!

FLIES

Time flies and all the flies are trying to get warm.
They're all over the house like bees in a swarm.
They're even on laundry that I hung out to dry. They light on your nose and your head as they fly!

I'm not an idiot who would save the common fly. I grin and take pleasure as they flop and they die.
I found a dead cat that was covered with flies, and buried him while hearing their damnable cries!

I may have imagined their buzz meant a thing…but I was very lucky they weren't bees who sting. Yes, flies are vermin here to test all our souls. There'll always be something… like gophers and moles.

FORGIVENESS

It's important to forgive and forget, but the process doesn't come easy. The human pride and spirit flinch…and even make one queasy!

When we get hurt or angry there is only one thing showing. It's pride that causes all the ruts in fields we may be sowing.

Pride can be good and can be bad and we can't survive without it, but the trouble is that the bad seems good, though we always defend or hide it!

Good pride is that which you feel when your children stand before you, and tell you they made great marks in school, and never just ignore you.

Bad pride is when we resist forgiveness and go stubbornly on our way. Later we feel guilty but spoiled everybody's day!

Forgiving comes really hard to us, but God says we must do it. Even though we may think we're right. If we don't we will surely rue it!

GOSSIP

According to the Bible the human tongue is a terrible weapon, worse than sword or any other.

I really have come to believe that perhaps with good intentions, people say things and pass on information that should be kept private. They cause much harm to others also through speaking half-truths!

Witness the leaking of facts that have no basis in truth by the media. What power they have and what a mess we have as a result. This becomes the fuel that separates people. It causes hatred and misunderstanding between races and individuals.

All this evil comes from snide and mean remarks that come from the human tongue! When I have a gripe I go directly to the person or organization involved. I never tell things behind other's backs, with one exception…the right to defend myself.

When things bother you, why not come right out in the open with them? The desire to be important may be behind the sickness called "Gossip".

HALFZEIMERS DISEASE

Sometimes when I go shopping and stand in the store and stare, at all the food around me…can't remember why I'm there!

And as I walk along the aisles it finally comes to me, that I came to just buy butter and milk…I'm getting old, you see.

The owners of the store keep moving everything around. It really drives me crazy for by habits I am bound.

They shift things around often so you'll buy a great deal more, and end up spending twice as much as you go out the door.

Oh, how I'd like the old times to come back when you could phone…the store and they'd deliver all your orders to your home.

There was also something friendly about the ice-man bringing ice, and the vegetables brought by horse and cart! Those days were awfully nice.

HERE'S TO TALKERS!

Without people who talk we never would have... anything but silence...how boring and sad. The whole thing is that you have something to say that's interesting and you would like to portray! There are those who sit pursing their lips just to show that you are not interesting to them, don't you know? Why don't they speak out, not just write their ideas...expressing them out loud to all waiting ears?

I think that they really don't have much to say, and haven't experienced lots in their day. Yes, they've been good parents and have lots of money, but they've never been out in the cruel world my honey! So here's to the talkers who share many things that they've found out in life with excitement it brings. Most who have lived their lives fully can be... a real threat to others and to powers that be! People who talk are anathema to those, who love their think tanks and many who pose, as great intellects...I'll take the talkers who have something to say, who've been out in the harsh world and the penalty pay. Writing about the real world's fine therapy, but living fully the life, is the real life for me!

THE REAL HEROES

For me, the hardest thing in life is to discover that those we always put on a pedestal and admired are not what they appeared to be. In other words, to find out that they were really pretenders, underneath all their outer show of sincerity.

In a way, it shows how gullible some of us are, not even attempting to see through the outer core and into the person's real being. I guess only God can do that! It is disillusioning to look up to your heroes and then find out that they really didn't deserve your admiration.

It is not the physical pains that come with old age that hurt the most. It is finding out the truth about your heroes, both close to you and those with great power. I always admired George Bush Senior, his wife and son. I no longer can, when I follow what they have done. Brushing all politics aside, I then have to examine my own life and self, and be honest about it.

I care not one wit what people think of me. I found out long ago that it really doesn't matter...what does matter is that I know my many faults, look them squarely in the face and try to change my attitudes that are plainly self-destructive. I also realize that beating up on yourself for past mistakes is wrong.

The best way is perhaps to consider my former heroes like the "Over-ripe Banana" over-do for tossing down the drain and flushing it well.

The REAL heroes are the ones who give their lives for others, never asking for anything in return. Those who quietly nurture others, the volunteers, and men and women who serve our country by risking their own lives. The great teachers, whose interest is in their students and not themselves. Devotion to duty is central to the cores of their beings. Being heads of this and that committee and always having the praise of those around them is not important to these, the real Heroes.

written 7/22/2004 by Alva Houston

HORSES

Today the bright sun shines on the snow, and it's reasonably warm…not thirty below.

I remember when I had horses and on cold days icicles stuck to their noses…this seemed not to faize!

When I let them out mornings in their field to run, they'd kick up their heels, looking like it was fun.

Those were happy days with them around, with their wonderful whinnies, that glorious sound!

People who don't like horses are crazy I think…for even their doo-doos have no awful stink!

Dedicated to Bay State Breeze.

HOW SAD

It's sad to see suffering of elders in years.

It's sad to see people end lives with their tears. But God has His reasons and we all have our fears, that perhaps we've even earned the pain that appears! Our pains reflect those of our Saviour and tell, that we're closer to Heaven and farther from Hell! I just hope God forgives us for all our mistakes as I really repent, whatever it takes.

36.
HUMOR AND PETS

If you haven't got humor you might as well die for it's awfully unfortunate age will not lie. When your looks have gone and your joints ache a lot, and you know that your brain is beginning to rot…just pick yourself up and put on a smile that will keep you alive… and stay for a while!

When your eyesight grows dim and wrinkles appear, just take a long walk with your doggie, my dear! Your animals love you though old you may be, and their love and devotion is enough, don't you see? Humans can fail you but an animal friend will be there beside you, right up to the end!

Written 4/4/2005 by Alva Houston

I BLAME THE MEDIA!

Everyday I listen to the voices of the journalists and wonder…How we ever made it in this world that pundits only plunder!

Instant gratification is the rule that all the media play. I refuse to listen to their lies and my common sense will stay!

The media, be it left or right has power beyond belief, so I stick to the rules of "right and wrong"
That give me some relief.

Their rules are to confuse us all…to make us just their tools! I broke away from them long ago because I see they're fools.

The few that try to talk real sense are left in left-field, so to speak! They haven't a snowball's chance in hell of telling the truth and leak…

just a little here and there and then go back to slosh… that they spout out or they will soon end up "out of Biz" by gosh!

ILLEGALS

My wonderful grandma came here, without hesitation or fear. To become an American from Sweden she came and traveled far across the Atlantic without shame! She came with a sponsor who put her to work –and from that in her lifetime she would never shirk. Not like those illegals who come to get welfare the minute they get in, they never WILL share.

They've learned that they can come through our borders at night and now we find ourselves in a real plight! They get all of our healthcare mostly scot free, while the rest of us pay through the nose, don't you see? Our country will never be what it was because our government (shame on it) is the real cause-of our becoming a third world nation for sure. In the end it intends that we all will be poor!

We are told that the world is more important than us, and the ones who have power don't want us to fuss. We are also told that we have nothing to say and we can't hold this globalization at bay. I, for one, am so glad that I'm really old, for if I were young I would fight cause I'm bold. I would stand up against all this illegal mess, and I'd probably end up in prison, I guess!

JAKE

Jake's a chow-husky. Believe me he's tough! We found out one evening when things became rough. I lay in my bed free from world and from mob, when Douglass came home very late from his job. All of a sudden I awoke to a loud sound that would scare anybody who happened around! I jumped from my slumber to find a bad scene, for Jake had Doug pressed to the wall and looked mean!

His teeth bared, his hair up, he was not the sweet dog I remembered that morning when still in a fog. What happened we can't know but I had a thought that policeman had come to our door and had sought some druggies whom they knew were living nearby. Jake is a real guard dog of quality high! If the police even yelled at him at the front gate he hadn't forgotten when Doug came home late. Doug wears a badge as all police do and I figure Jake saw it and got in a stew!

In the dark bedroom Doug must have tripped on his tail. Jake was half asleep, but this caused his wail! The weather has been rainy for ages it seemed and the dog was still all male when he became mean! The lesson is this: Do have your male dogs fixed very early…and if you have a chow you must do it REALLY!

JUSTIFICATION

Life seems at times to be an exercise in futility! As I approach the end of it, I pray constantly to retain my faith in Jesus Christ. I have to depend on the ideas that have been implanted in my mind over many years. I still (being a sinner saved by grace and a leap of faith) question why I am here at all! I AM human.

I am convinced, despite my questions, that no man will ever create seeds which give life to everything! Therefore, I personally believe there HAS to be a Master Plan! Man creates such wonders in technology, in medicine and the arts that it would be the ultimate conceit to think that there is no superior brain working behind the scenes and in our lives.

Christianity is the only religion that states that we are ALL sinners and need redemption. It states that God is the spirit of love, and the love of money is the root of all evil! Chanting five times a day whether you are a Muslim or follow Buddha or any other religion that follows strict rules and regulations will get you nowhere. We are all in the same boat and as the Bible teaches " there is no one good...no, not one" and accepting God's Son, Jesus is the leap of faith demanded by a Holy God!

LARKSPUR

Three years ago, at least, someone gave me a plastic bag full of small seeds. They looked like pepper, and she didn't even know what they were! They had been left behind when people moved out of her apartment.

The first year they came up and didn't get very tall but produced beautiful pink, white and purple blossoms. I took some to the nursery and the owner pronounced them "Larkspur". Being interested in gardening from youth I remembered that was the wild cousin to the Delphinium. That is a very tall and beautiful blossoming plant.

To this day their humble cousins grace our garden with their beauty! They take over and need little water. Just brush up the seeds and throw them around! Each year they come up even in cracks in cement along our walk.

I call them a gift from God. The dominant color is now purple, however. The other colors are weaken and we have almost none, however the plants get 5 ft. tall!

LIFE'S SURPRISES

I will never cease to wonder at what life has in store for me! Here at the age of 78 I'm reminded of how strong Love can be.

Over this amazing computer I heard from a new friend, whose uncle was my first love, a love that couldn't bend.

Cal Burrows was the boy's name, who left us all early in his life…in the second World War that caused much pain and strife. He was killed in the Normandy invasion before even reaching the beach. We who loved him hold him in our hearts, though through death we cannot reach.

Yet, something strange is working over miles and over years…to bring people together despite their
Woes and tears. Yes, God is working in lives of all who've loved and lost somehow. He's getting us ready to meet Him and past loves we think of now!

Written this day, the 25th of January, 2005
By Alva Houston

MY DEAR DOCTOR

Our doctor is unusual in this world of money grabbers. He puts up with all patients, even with the silly crabbers! He, when exhausted with government rules, paperwork, and regulations, still carries on with this work you'd don't find in other nations.

We're losing good men everyday…can't take this awesome job. They get worn out and just give up…for this I really sob. What they need is for all of us to tell them just how great they are. How we appreciate what they do for us, we know it near and far.

For all who suffer pain, like me, we see what he is bearing. We owe these dedicated much for all their care and caring. Too few thank doctors for their skills and their dedication, but I simply thank Tom Watson. He's a hero in our nation! His staff is always helpful too and deserves so many thanks from all of us who depend on them, we salute their many ranks!

OUR CATS

Once upon a time there were three cats who never bothered hunting or caught rats.

Their names are Tuffy, Muffie and dear Kitty and always get down to the nitty-gritty!

Each morning when the time's exactly five, they wake me up telling me I'm alive! They meow and chase me to their bowl, demand their food and test my soul.

Even though at times I'd like to sleep…under my bed covers they will creep,

And stick me just a little with claws or knead me with their softer paws.

I find they are a lot of fun, and visit with them til' we see the sun.

It's good they make me feel alive, but back to bed I often dive! I love these kitties though they are demanding and study their habits, mind expanding. I see they're smarter than we think. From what they want they never shrink. I've learned a lot from our dear cats, even if at times they drive me bats!

OUR MIRACLE PEACH TREE
(Dedicated to those who don't believe in God)

Five years ago when Doug and I still were playing golf once in a while, a nice man who lived on the golf course gave us some peaches from his tree. We ate them with relish and I threw their pits out back in our garden. I never thought of it again until a year later two small sprouts came up, one deformed. I ruthlessly tore it out and left the other.

Again, I never paid any attention to our new friend, nor did I fertilize it. I left it to survive alone and checked on it once in a while. I did go out and talk to it frequently. This year that little fellow is fifteen feet high and gave us it's first four beautiful free-stone peaches! I call that a real miracle, don't you? Remember, I never even covered that peach pit!

PAINTING

My sister had such talent for painting, I must say…her work was unbelievably good, but she later turned to clay.

She made darling little animals and things from imagination. Rheumatoid arthritis hit her as so many in our nation. I wish she'd stuck to oils and watercolors, but she loved the wheel and clay so much. She must have loved the feel of clay being something she could touch!

I am so sorry that she has suffered so with crippled hands so sore… and aches and pains from arthritis…they are an awful bore!
I join her now with my backaches that threaten to do me in…but we keep going Ellie, don't we, with a smile and with a grin!

POEMS

These poems come from inner thoughts from can't be sure, "just where"! Probably they come from a life which gave me lots of things to bear. I've had cancer, disc troubles, the shingles and heart op. However the mind's still active and these ideas never stop.

I've been criticized for being an opinionated lady. I can't help over a lifetime that I see the good and shady! These days you're supposed to agree with everybody else. Don't you dare be an individual. You'll be put upon the shelf, where the people can forget you and ridicule you too. What a sad state of affairs we have that we may in future rue!

When I was small I loved to listen to my elders then, for I realized they knew more than I in this world of men, and women who had struggled bravely to come to the USA. Their guts I do admire still and the price one has to pay…for the precious freedom that we have and now take so for granted. Those patriots got down and kissed the soil when their ships landed!

THIS IS A PRECEDENT!

My Lord…what have we come to as a people in this country? Yes, this is about the precedent we are setting in the murdering deliberately of an innocent woman, Terri Schiavo.

When my mother was dying at the age of 80 after a major stroke I was accused of wanting to kill her because I saw the feeding tube as just a prolongation of her life for the money the doctors and hospital could make! I knew that hydration was important because otherwise the patient suffers real agony in dying. This is what I was told at least!

Now judges have ALL POWER to decide who lives and dies! These so-called "mercy killings" will become commonplace if this precedent is followed. This is a good way to get rid of unwanted expenses of medicare and social security, isn't it? No more old grandparents sitting around and passing on some values to others…but of course few consider values anyway these days, do they?

RIGHTEOUS ANGER

Right now I have a welling up inside, and an anger I can never hide! When sitting in the Doctor's office today there sat two Spanish speaking women for whom we all will pay.

Both were pregnant with other kids with them there. For our language and our culture they seem not to care. Across our borders and encouraged every day...by President Bush and politicians...but we Americans have to Pay!

Out here the anger mounts, and mounts to no avail. We protest to the winds and rain and even to the gale. What's wrong with putting thousands of citizens on the border. This may be the only way we'll get some Law and Order!

There's bound to be a civil war again. Innocents will suffer for this madness. We embrace disease and terrorists. We take them in with gladness! The day is coming when the people will eventually see, that this invasion spells doomsday for you, my friend,and me.

So what do real legitimate citizens really do...to protect themselves and survive through this crazy, and planned zoo? There's blood-letting coming. I say you can be sure of that...and civil war where nobody will know who's good and who's a rat!

Written 3/14/2003

SEEDS

Having written about seeds before I don't mean to bore! I just feel I must talk about them some more.

We go through life thinking that man is very smart. Along the way we forget that something else is a part...of everything we have and are...the lowly seed! Without it we wouldn't have a thing that we need.

The seed makes all life and ourselves included. How come we are so dumb and often so deluded. To make man the highest intelligence that exists, is the ignorance of man and woman that persists!

All around we see there is a high intelligence at work (in our lives and others) but we tend to shirk the facts right before us. It's sad and stupid not to see that there HAS to be a Creator of you and me!

Dedicated to those who have yet to see the Light.
I pray they will!

Written March 2,2005

51.
SOUR PICKLE VERSUS SWEET

Some are those who are sour in their approach to all the people. They believe they're superior to everyone, from their lofty, lofty steeple.

They look down on others if they happen to be different from them, and offer very little to this world of many men. Like the sour pickle which disapproves especially of the sweet, they'll go their way in history distaining most they meet.

It's too bad they cannot see into the beauty of all types.
Those who are out-going really give them lots of hypes! So leave them all to Heaven, is all that we can do. Both pickles will be eaten in the end...that happens to be true.

The sweetest of the pickles will leave us with a sweeter taste, while the sour one will leave us with a grimace on our face!

THANKSGIVING

I remember so well the turkey and the dressing and the smell, of pies sitting cooling. I remember them so well! I remember all the laughter and the conversations full of Swedish accents in our family...and of the strangest pull, of traditions that are gone today amid cacophony, of the noisy noisy rappers and their angry poetry!

Tradition served to bind us to each other in some ways. How I long for all the warmth and love from those remembered days. The present seems divisive to those of us who would return to a family's sense of honor, and some butter we could churn...to the ice-cream made from churning with some jimmies on the top...to balloons we used to blow up and have great fun to pop!

THE AMERICANS

When our people were faced with World War 2 we did without things and some freedom too! We all knew then what were the costs, and we faced them with all the brave men that we lost!

I lost two dear friends who were only nineteen.
These brave boys, whose thoughts were also so clean. In those days almost everyone treasured the morals that made our country great… to them go the laurels!

Today there is a selfishness across our dear land.
That leads to destruction of a people at hand.
We no longer think of each other unselfishly, for
We're consumed by "what WE want" and much more I see!

I fear for my country if we are self-centered. I fear for the consequences that seem to have entered, for we'll pay high prices that I always called FREEDOM, if we keep on this path and never even see 'em!

54.
THE DIFFERENCE BETWEEN "LIBERAL", "PROGRESSIVE", "SOCIALIST", "COMMUNIST", AND "FASCIST".

There is really no difference between these "ists", in practical application! Many long years ago the leftists ... whether they were dedicated to bringing about a dictatorship of the whole world under the United Nations, or just their dupes, realized that words and labels such as "communist"are repugnant to most free Americans. They deliberately changed their rhetoric

To "Globalization" and appealed to the ignorance of young people who have been brainwashed by the term "Citizens of the world"! Such a wonderful concept is it not? The only trouble is that you have to give up your freedom, your borders, and eventually your sovereignty.

No longer has the United States got borders, and sad to say, the hard working Americans are paying through the nose for the undermining of our blessed free system. The Constitution is called "a flexible document" by none other than Ruth Bader Ginsberg, Supreme Court Justice! She is the former head of the American Civil Liberties Union" which was set up to defend communists way back in the fifties, I believe. Our immigration laws had been undermined allowing communists to come here and become citizens! Remember that communists are dedicated to the over-throw of our free Republic.

The capitalist system may not be perfect, but it is the best ever created to allow individual liberty. The sad thing is that the push to get citizens to give up their right to bear arms will spell the end of our freedom and our ability to defend ourselves. The leftists have managed to disarm many countries and their crime rates have gone through the roof.

We are fighting a battle of the mind…and unfortunately we are losing. I have to ask myself what has happened to the people's ability to see through the danger in "Open Borders"! Just that alone shows that we really have no country at all. Patrick Henry said long, long ago "Give me liberty or give me death". That's the way I feel, especially since my friends died for freedom in WW2.

THE HANDSHAKE

One day long ago we answered an Ad for a house to rent. Our dog had to be leashed and the landlord of the house we lived in was an unpleasant man who promised things and never delivered. No screens for the windows, no hood over the stove…pretty basic things for any home were never upcoming!

Looking in the local paper we found an ad for a two bedroom for rent. We called and met the owner the very same day! With a handshake we closed the deal…no contract, no nothing…just a firm handshake! This is the way business used to be done, but we never expected it these days.

Our relationship with Dan Porter was wonderful over 11 years. He was a kind and gentle man that we will always think of, with the regret that he's no longer with us! We lost him to cancer. He was much younger than we are. His wife has taken on the job of looking after their properties, and is a pretty good example of feminine "GUTS"! She fixed our plumbing when it went askew and was bent and determined to do it herself!

We wanted to leave these few words in praise of a humble and nice human who is mightily missed and his wife who keeps going with a smile! Thank you Dan and Dee.

THE SELF

When the heart has been broken the hurt last so long. Though a person may try and knows that it's wrong, this thing called our feelings will fight to the end, our pride to bolster and to defend.

It's our survival that seems to make us go on. We will carry this burden until we are gone. Each day we may fight it, the "self" that is us. Let's pray when we die we won't make a fuss. Let's go to our maker without guilt, without pain, and live on forever…a new life to gain!

Dedicated to those who mistakenly think the afterlife will be boring…on a cloud perhaps!

THE SNOWS ARE HERE

I sit at my window watching the snow as it falls so steadily, and I know it will bring needed water in desert mountains. It's purer and better than comes from fountains. I thank God for snow and the water it brings to our dry and parched land through the rivers and springs.

Some people stay home when they can't drive around. Maybe that's good for a while they found some higher power controls weather we must admit... that we control little, but don't worry a bit! Stop worrying about what you eat and you wear, for we're all in those hands and rely on His care.

Just look out your window and marvel my friend at the beauty He's sent us for it may soon end. The roads will be slippery, the snow will turn brown when we finally get out and drive into town. Just try to remember the purest of white, that falls to the earth...what a beautiful sight!

A TRUE SIGN

One night many years ago, desperation reached and nowhere to go…I asked the Lord if He was real and to His being made appeal! Raised as a pagan I heard of Him, but thought that faith was just a whim. I lived 55 years in darkness before the seed of faith came into my core.

I hung my head with a gun in hand…thinking humans were a sorry band and why should God, if He were there even care for us or answer prayer? He gave an answer to my plea to know the truth…a sign to me!

A black thunderstorm had been going on…for hours it pounded every house and lawn. For hours it whirled throughout the day. Beside my side my gun still lay! I hung my head and clasped the gun…but when I looked up there was the sun. In that instant clouds parted by His grace, and the sun was shining in my face!

Perhaps you may not all agree with the sign that God had given me. I've been tested through many many trials that the devil gives us with his wiles. The Lord has always seen me through. I can only wish the same for you!

59.
INSTEAD OF THE "FACT OF THE MATTER", HOW ABOUT THE TRUTH OF IT?

It's the middle of the night and here I am again with many thoughts buzzing through my head like the bees I see in my beautiful plants. Having degenerating discs plagueing me, plus my eyesight going and most of all, plain old age, I have done a lot of soul-searching lately. I have always been careful to examine myself and my motivations for doing things. Writing thoughts down gives one the opportunity of doing just that, and I think it's important to examine one's own self. At least the Bible teaches that the heart can be desperately "Wicked" and that we can fool ourselves!

When you turn 78 somehow everything does look very black at times, and I have been accused of being negative by some that I thought of as friends most of my life. The "truth" is that I have been a cockeyed optimist and loved life's experiences for the most part. There are good times, bad times and in between times for all of us, I believe, and the trick is to get through them without being bitter! I believe I have managed that. Being hard on yourself is very good in it's effect. It is the root of humility!

There comes a time, when one HAS to face the unpleasant facts squarely. To be truthful and honest with yourself, you have to face death, the ultimate truth for all of us. I am prepared for that and glad that I have faith in a God who loves us all. Self-examination has been important to me. The question is always, "Why do I write, paint, cartoon, play the piano and sing (badly now)? I find comfort in these pursuits as I believe talent is GIVEN to us when we are born and should be used, shared, and that giving is the most important thing anyone of us can do.

One has to face the ultimate alone as when we entered this world. I have prepared myself for that going out of it as well, and that seems like a victory in itself.

Pain has been easier for me than most and I've gotten used to it. My many operations have never taken away my spirit to keep trying. Although I know that many people feel I am too out-spoken, I have expressed my most inner-felt ideas and opinions, and have no regrets about it. I have never done it to hurt anyone or for selfish reasons. Those I loved I felt would understand this.

"The rain falls on the just and unjust alike" the Word of God says. Facing disillusionment is harder than facing pain. I now realize that expecting people to really understand each other is impossible...that is, without Christ. I now see that I have expected too much, too much even from myself. Now I will always just give thanks for everything I've been given and still have, and leave the rest to "Heaven" where all will be understood.

written 7/ 27/ 2004 by Alva Houston

THE TSUNAMI

All of sudden it seems that mankind is becoming more aware of how helpless we all are in the universal scheme of things!

I, for one, think of our own Mt. Shasta which hasn't stirred for 200 or more years. When will the forces of nature stir it and show us once more that we really control very little.

I look at the seed, which creates ALL life and everything we have. Even the great scientists could not create one seed! Until man accomplishes this, I will cling to my faith and marvel at the power that does control the universe.

Common sense seems to be lacking among the intelligentsia and aetheism runs rampant among the groups that meet in "Think-tanks" and preach secularism. It would be a good idea for them to consider the SEED and realize that everything they have comes from it!

THE WISDOM OF AGE

Some deny that age brings wisdom at all! I have known some pretty stupid elders who spend all their time either sitting at the senior center gossiping, or watching the boob-tube.

Now I'm not bragging but everyday brings me some kind of goal. I think people ought to have goals right up to the end of their lives. Perhaps this process has to start in childhood.

I remember when I was very young I thought that if I wasn't disciplined, I would never accomplish anything! My grandmother (Mormor) had a saying that comes into my mind often. She used to say "Strength doesn't grow on feather pillows"! SHE was one of the wise ones.

LOST LOVES

There are so many lost loves…Mother, Father, loves, Grandparents, Uncles and Aunts, friends, Animals …dogs, cats, birds and horses! So many times I think of them all, and hope that I will see them in the afterlife I believe in.

If this life is simply a vapor as some believe and there is no hereafter, it would seem stupid to have lived at all. All the troubles, mistakes, pain and learning would mean absolutely nothing in the universe of time.

I prefer to have taken a leap of faith based on being a gardener over many years. No man, including the greatest scientists like Einstein, has ever created one seed, much less all which create everything we have. Think about it…all we have on the earth was created from seed!

Dedicated to my grandmother, Olga Kjellmark

63.
THROW OUT THE BUMS!

Amazed at the Senators who still reign supreme, I wonder how the public votes them back again and ageen! It shows how little interest the public has… in politics…and a congress full of gas.

I for one look at the motley crew, that steal taxpayers money and like the birds flew…
Back to their states to fool the folks before their being finally croaks!

They disgust me, these selfish evil bums. I wouldn't, from my table even give them crumbs!

TIME

Today's time is the 24th of January, 2005! Where it all has gone is a mystery to me. Everyday goes more quickly it seems and when you reach your 79th year it really goes fast!

I am grateful for each day that I live without pain as I have a serious back condition. I have discovered that Chiropractors help me more than anyone else. I can remember them being considered quacks years ago. I am sure they did everything the same way they do now. What a shame that they had to struggle so hard to be recognized! Time has changed all that for the better.

At this late stage of life I appreciate their talents so much. It takes time to make one accepted and the Chiropractors spend 7 years before getting their licenses. That is a great deal of training time.

It also takes a lot of time to write, to observe things to write about and to be recognized as a writer of some quality. Writing things down helps the brain to keep functioning and I believe that most people who do it only pursue it out of necessity! To be published is not important. It is complicated and a real hassle as well. Making money has to be the publisher's main interest I suppose, but in the old days it wasn't necessary to invest your own money to get your works out in the public. Today, it seems to be almost impossible to get any publisher interested in your
Work no matter what it is! The world is consumed with making money to the point that writers, and artists of any kind have to almost do it themselves. Time has changed all things so much that the world is completely different from when I was young. The Americans still are the greatest people in the world and time has not changed that! They seek to help everyone in disasters and time has not changed their basic goodness while those they have helped in the rest of the world seem not to do anything but criticize!

TODAYS' KIDS

My blood boils when I see kids throw their paper cups in the street! When you ask them to please pick up their trash they tell you to "F…off!" This is what has happened to manners and just plain decent behavior in the USA of 2005.

I saw the Hitler Youth in the making and I believe I'm seeing the same things happening here that happened in Germany in the late thirties. The kids are encouraged to think they know more than the grownups. The next step will be to organize them!

I must say that the schools and the parents are partly responsible for this development, but the MEDIA bears most of the blame. They feed the worst possible scenarios to everyone from early morning to late at night…sex, violence, and disgusting language!

I can't recognize the decent parents and teachers that we knew and respected in the present day lot.
The ones that are worth their weight in Gold dare not speak out for the most part.

66.
TOO MUCH INFORMATION!
And too little common sense.

What a curse the television has become. You can understand why the strict Muslims and Radical religious groups point at us as the great satan!

Our Television features young girls gone wild, baring breasts, shaking bottoms in invitation, and generally acting like street whores.

Our ads feature Viagra and several other wonderful sex drugs that can even give you an erection for four hours!

We show ads for lawyers, (the scum of the earth in my opinion,) willing to fight for anything you might have wrong with you that was caused by some wealthy company.

We have entertainers on late at night discussing their fight to overcome their drugs habits….their broken marriages and all their troubles in general! Ye Gods, are these people representative of our nation as a whole? I don't think they are, but I'll hazard a guess the radical America haters do!

Why don't we ever hear anything good about what is happening in Iraq or Afghanistan? Or why don't we ever hear the good that is going on right here at home? Obviously the powers that be don't think GOOD sells! I for one am sick of all Television with two exceptions, Animal planet and the History Channel.

During WW2 you had a report of the huge number of casualties only infrequently. Now, the news carries daily tolls of every boy or girl killed and somehow doesn't tell you how many of the Iraqi troops suffered casualties! They never miss telling you how many civilians are killed, though!

Can't you see how we are being set up as the bad guy who deserves to be blown off the face of the earth. Witness this Churchill character who teaches at the University of Colorado and is surely the biggest America-hater there is. To say that we need more 9-11s is treason in my opinion. Freedom of speech doesn't extend to crying "Fire" in a theater when there's no fire… so why does it extend to these sedious traitors! This shows how far we have fallen and how easily the Americans with any guts have been shut up. The double standard is in power and if you're a patriot, you are also a right wing extremist, a racist, a noodle brain and not worthy of the media's time! I think that about covers my opinions and I feel better getting them out of my system. Most Americans are afraid of speaking out on any subject. That's how successful the propaganda war has been over my lifetime…78+ years!

TROUBLE

"Trouble" is a kitty with big blue eyes! His mother came from Siamese I surmise. He sat in the middle of a garbage can top, friend put out for thirty wild cats, he didn't stop... eating...never afraid of the mob of bigger cats who earned their food from catching rats.

Trouble was half the size of them, but brave as the very best of men. He captured my heart and I took him home to Doug who I got right on the phone. I told him this kitten was special so... Doug agreed to take one mo! (We already had three great cats)

Trouble doesn't ever purr, and he thinks he's a dog, from your feet won't stir. He follows Doug when he mows the lawn and when they're finished
He does a yawn, and lies beside Jake, our Husky-chow, to whom he's a buddy and doesn't bow.

I have never had a cat like him, and we got him strictly on a whim!

TRUE FRIENDS

Throughout our lives we learn to see that friendship means much to you and me!

When money is a problem too, real friends can help us to get through.

When to the doctors we must run, at break of day or when the sun goes down, we'll find our friends are there, for they're the ones who really care!

So here's to the true ones that we treasure whose loyalty is beyond our measure,

TUFFY

Tuffy is a big long-haired yellow cat who weighs 38 pounds. He waddles along as he makes his rounds! If his bowl isn't full he meows loud-ly. His voice is so high he can reach high C!

We had him fixed when just a tot, and he sticks close to home an awful lot. In fact he likes me as his only pal, and runs under the bed when another gal come to the door and enters in. He's bonded to me, even licks my chin.

I comb his thick fur almost everyday and he rolls around with a smile so gay, as I comb his tummy and comb his back, He's a wonderful kitty and that's a fact. There's not a mean bone in his body or face and I love him dearly with his cheerful grace.

I think about leaving him when I die, as he may live longer…and I cry! For I wonder what will become of him, my dear friend Tuffy and his sister, Muffie.

WHAT EVEN HAPPENED TO HUMOR AND MUSIC?

As I observe life's changing scene there are two things I really miss! The first is good music coming out in the 2000s…the other is a sense of humor amongst the younger crowd.

The music is very depressing these days. When I was in my teens the songs were about romance and hope. Now they are about perversion and hopelessness.

You have to look at a society influenced by television! That's where all the ideas seem to come from. I turn to my sound system and either play recorded music from way back or produce it myself.

As far as humor…don't see much of that these days. Everyone seems to have a cloud of gloom hanging over them. I talk to volumes of people and they all seem depressed, instead of fighting mad at the way things are going.

In my usual humble opinion I think everyone ought to be picketing theaters, schools, and everyone who is pushing for government control
over everything we do! My sense of humor tells me that the dumbest people run most of the government and that they ought to be thrown out of office in an ignominious way…tarred and feathered the way it used to be done!

I can see certain Senators going out of town with feathers all over them, can't you? How about the ones who have been in office for over 4 decades?

I wonder if a particularly stupid man I'm thinking of would be wagging his finger at all of us over TV then?????

71.

WHAT THE HECK!

"What the heck" is what you say when things don't go right everyday. After all there is another, another day in which you'd ruther… do some work on paintings started as from household chores you darted.

There are real compensations to old age which people don't often see. The fact that you don't have to rush to work and you can even be…really relaxed about each day and have the time to do a lot of fun things that happen to be creative too!

So folks, if you live long enough and passed youth swiftly by…don't worry about your liver spots and wrinkles that don't lie. They tell you that you're on in years, so what and "what the heck"
Grateful that you're living still…don't be a sour wreck!

72.
WHAT'S IT ALL ABOUT ALVIE?

I wish I knew folks, but I think the more you know makes more to know! Opinions change over the years, and who knows how many lies we have all believed in a lifetime.

One thing I cling to is that our lives are meaningful. We are here to learn and to give is all I can get out of the experience of living. Every life comes to a stop at some time. It would be a frightening prospect if you believed that we are just "Dust in the Wind" as the song says.

Wishful thinking brings you to faith and why we have any. I certainly have no faith in mankind seeing the cruelty it perpetuates! Maybe that's why the leap of faith in Christ came easy to me.
I never blamed God for things because I saw that most evil comes from man and is passed on by him (meaning women as well).

I am here to learn more and to give more is the way I see it! The end IS in sight but I couldn't go another day without my faith...and would blow my head off immediately...for life wouldn't have meant a thing...just a useless exercise in futility!

WHY I WRITE AT ALL!

Why write at all you all may ask? I'll say that it's an addictive task. It's also results from my frustration at what's now happening to our nation! I write to get things off my chest, but my sense of humor creates the rest. Just read if you wish an old gal's thinking and even though you find yourself shrinking... from my firm ideas remember they come from fun and fears!

They say that if we ignore History...we'll repeat mistakes...endlessly. I hope these tomes just give you thought about many battles we won and fought. Some are funny and some are not!

All written between the years 2003 and 2004
By Alva Houston

WORK

I thank God for work and projects every day. I can't understand how people can sit on their behinds and watch TV all day when they get old.

My dear grandmother (on the Swedish side of the family) always taught us kids a lot of very deep lessons with simple sayings such as: "Strength doesn't grow on feather pillows" and " It's not work that kills you, but worrying!" We called this wonderful and wise woman "Mormor" which means mother's mother.

Mormor's father died and left his wife with eleven kids during a bad drought. The farm could barely feed them, so the eldest, my grandmother got a sponsor in the USA and crossed the dangerous Atlantic to become an American citizen. It took her years to learn English and pass all the legal tests and requirements to become truly an "American", but she did it with pride. We allow illegals to come in today and get welfare and free medical treatment which is killing our medical system, but Mormor earned her right to become the loyal American she was. How far we have fallen since those days.

WORST GRIPES

Over a lifetime I've heard the phrase "Never talk politics or religion" and it annoys the heck out of me! In the first place those two subjects are probably the most important to discuss with anyone who has an IQ of more than 100. How on earth have the American people been sold on this nincompoop idea?

I'll tell you why and how. The brainwashing job has been constant. Believe me when I tell you that back when our forefathers were struggling to introduce a new way of looking at freedom and survival they argued night and day over how to form a constitution that would protect us from tyrants and dictatorship.

Discussion today has evolved to "small talk" in other words "drivel"! I've been told that is the basis of friendship and I disagree heartily. There is no friendship if you have to hide your opinions and resort to discussing the weather, or how you feel and how you are doing in general. We all can look out the window and see the weather, and we don't need to discuss all the details of our lives…that's selfish. What we need to discuss are the very things that AFFECT our lives and freedom. Shallowness is cowardess in my opinion whether it comes from loved ones or strangers or friends. That is the direction my beloved USA has been going ever since the 60s generation was born. Many don't realize that if you don't discuss important events and historic ones you may have to fight for your lives with weapons against the powerful government we have created because we wouldn't face and discuss these things! Oh well, there probably will be no weapons available to you when the mighty Washington moguls get finished planning the "Hate Crimes" bills they are working on now. Canada has already got their people to accept this monstrous idea.

You won't even be able to express any disagreement with those in power or you'll be slapped in prison or worse! I, for one would rather be dead! It seems that "Give me liberty or give me death" was a famous quote from way back when people DID express their strong opinions and that was accepted. No way will people now discuss any important subjects. They are spoiled and soft compared to our forefathers!

Written this 15th day of april…when you will have to pay your unfair taxes. This is also due to our unwillingness to fight against tyranny.

THE GOOD OL' DAYS

Those were the days well remembered, when we could never be dismembered. We stood as Americans by each other. Through thick and thin that none could smother!

Today there are those who would divide. I say their ways I can't abide. In World War 2 our boys stood tall and served, each one, his country's call.

How long can we survive like this? Those days many surely miss. If we to evil do give in, we'll stand in judgement for this sin. History will judge us that's for sure. Our beloved land will end up poor!

We'll pay a heavy price I fear for wrong courses we often steer. So let us stick together now, and to all evils never bow. Politics leads to selfishness and got us in this awful mess!

Printed in the United States
33441LVS00005B/298-300

9 781413 779943